# CONTENTS

I0134410

# DEDICATION

I am proud to dedicate this book to a number of people. I am the product of an amazing God-fearing village. They say it takes a village to raise a child. I thank God for my village, my family, every day. First, I give Glory and honor to my Lord and Savior, Jesus Christ. Without you, none of this would be possible. You continually find ways to bless me and my family, even when we are undeserving. Thank you for blessing me with this vision to share with others, and I pray you do with it, what you please, to honor and glorify You.

I dedicate this book to my wife, who not only loves me unconditionally, but has faith in what I do and supports me 100%. She is my rock, my foundation, and the person I lean on. Thank you for believing in me, and seeing the dream in me.

I also thank my parents for all the sacrifices they made in their own lives to provide for me. You have always believed there was something special about me. I pray that I make you proud.

To my students, who inspire me to do so much more with my life. You teach me how to be a better person every day and I can only hope that you have learned as much from me as I have from you.

And to my unborn baby girl. When you read this, I hope you understand how much I love you and want the best for you and other young people like you. Thank you for being such a blessing and a gift to my life. Daddy loves you!

Thank you for taking the time to read my book, Bus 23: Tips and Strategies to Help Teens Overcome Peer Pressure. It means the world that you have chosen to support this dream and I hope you are blessed beyond measure as a result.

With Love in Christ,

Coach

"When you come on tough times, you could cower and flee, play the background, or be the best you can be"

~Devon "Coach" Buchanan

# INTRODUCTION

I once heard a man say, "Your life is quotable too," meaning that you can live your life by quotes that you believe in. I knew I had to come up with a quote for my life. Something I truly believe: *"When you come on tough times, you could cower and flee, play the background, or be the best you could be."*

I didn't realize when I wrote this quote, how it would become a quote by which I could truly live my life. I got used to trying to play the background and just fit in, rather than standing out and shining the way God intends us all to do. See, as a young teen growing up in southwest Philadelphia, being bullied, picked on, and teased, I felt like I would be in school for the rest of my life. I never seemed to have much to look forward to, and as I got older, decisions got much harder to make. The more I started to value my relationships with other people the worse those decisions became. I believe many of you may be in the same situation.

Growing up, I also struggled to find the benefit in school, other than the fact that my parents told me I had to go, and my friends were there. I wanted to do well. I knew I was *supposed* to do well, but I didn't know *WHY*. I believe it's important to find your "why?" No one can give you a "why?", it must come from you, from deep within.

My name is Devon Buchanan, but to my students, family, co-workers and close friends, I'm known as "Coach". My students started calling me "Coach" as an easier way to refer to me around school rather than "Mr. Buchanan". It stuck as I began to grow as a man and become the person that people close to me trust and come to for advice and counsel. I believe God saw fit to bless me with the gifts of discernment and empathy. I use these traits to make the lives of the people around me better daily; but it wasn't always this way.

Don't get me wrong, I was a good kid, as I am sure you were and maybe still are, but as much as I wanted to do well, for some reason, trouble always found me. I kept getting caught in situations I didn't want to be in, doing things I didn't want to do or believe in doing. But before any change can happen, it is important to recognize when change is necessary.

Regardless of where you are in your life, I wrote this book to help equip you with the mindset and strategies to deal with negativity, unwanted peer-pressure, and achieve the goals you have set for yourself. I just-so-happens that the setting is a me on a school bus. Now here's the problem. Most people get information, but lack one crucial element: execution. Once you are given the tools, you must put them to use to build a strong foundation.

Of course, I already know what you're thinking: "How can you ACTUALLY help me achieve my goals?" It's simple really: three letters, when inserted into your everyday life, and everyday tasks, will change your belief of what you are truly capable. If you follow these three simple steps, you can achieve every goal you set a plan to accomplish. It will give you the confidence to ignore negativity and strive to be your best. Today, I'm going to ask you to B-E-T on yourself. The B-E-T system is powerful but meant to be easy to remember. B-E-T stands for:

**B - Believe in yourself and your ability to do your best**

**E - Encourage yourself when no one else will**

**T - Take your time, make the best decision**

I created this because I lacked confidence in who I was as an adolescent, and as an adult, I needed something easy to could remember that I could turn to when times get rough; and boy do times get rough. Of all the challenges in my life, my mind provided most of them. It was my inability to recognize that I was in my own way. I wanted to blame everyone else for things that happened to me, instead of taking ownership. You HAVE to self-assess. I couldn't recognize when the devil was at work in my life, trying to block the blessings that God had for me.

As a child, it's so hard to think about your future, especially when you're unsure of the present. It's difficult to understand that the work you're doing today, is to set yourself up for the success you want to have tomorrow. I finally decided to pair my childhood experiences as a young man growing up in Philadelphia and tough times on the school bus, with lessons I've learned as a veteran educator and put them into a book specifically for teens. If there's one thing I've learned it's that childhood and adolescence are challenging: challenging enough that you can't and shouldn't have to go through them on your own.

A strong sense of **self-esteem** and **self-concept** are two things that young people, particularly adolescence, struggle with developing until they are older. Self-esteem is defined as "confidence in one's own worth and abilities". Self-concept is a bit more complicated. It is defined as "the view you have of yourself physically, mentally, and socially." Most adolescents are bombarded with thoughts questioning their self-concept and how they view themselves. "Am I smart enough to score proficient on the PSSA?" "Why did she tag me on instagram?" These thoughts are the limiting thoughts in our self-talk that negatively affect how we view ourselves. There are several factors that affect the development of self-esteem, which in turn affects your ability to view yourself positively. In fact, some teens work hard to show a high level of self-esteem with an equally low level of self-concept. In other words, "talk the talk" but can't "walk the walk".

I'm excited to share with you some of the outrageous stories that had both a positive and negative effect on my self-esteem and self-concept. The negativity affected my growth and development as a young man, and it prevented me from being the best version of myself and ultimately what God wanted me to be. On the other hand, when I think about all the lessons I have learned from that negativity, and how they are now the positives in my life, I am reminded that, "It's not what you go through, it's how you come through." Say to yourself, "I am happy with where I am but more excited about where I'm going".

Now, you might be thinking, "Coach, why did you struggle with your self-esteem?" Well, I'm glad you asked! I would like for you to reminisce with me. Think back to your early years. I'm going to take you back to my early days of elementary and middle school. I'm going to take you back to the days of the school bus, my school bus, Bus 23…well…Philadelphia 4523 to be exact. It was on the school bus where I learned several lessons about life, I just didn't know how to apply them until now. That doesn't mean I should have waited until now to learn it. I enjoy thinking back on the things I've learned and watching them play out in my own life. For that reason, I can't wait to share this information with you. I want to help young people.  I want to help those who may be going through some of the same situations I went through growing up and provide them with strategies to overcome the moments that make adolescence seem like it will never end.

# "You must be willing, at any moment, to give up who you are, for what you will become"

# ~Dr. Eric Thomas
# (World's #1 Motivational Speaker)

# Lesson #1

# The importance of Self-Esteem and Self-Concept

How you feel about yourself has a significant effect on your character. The problem is, many teenagers base how they feel about themselves on how others view them. If they are viewed favorably by their peers, then they feel good about themselves. The opposite is also true. If they are viewed unfavorably by their peers, then they typically have lower **self-esteem**, resulting in a negative **self-concept.**

*"Too many people overvalue what they are not and undervalue what they are."*

*~Malcolm Forbes*

*(Forbes Magazine)*

What does this quote mean to you?

# Chapter 1

## NOT A CARE IN THE WORLD

I carefully stepped up with my right foot, then my left, then my right foot again. I turned to the left, and there it was, a sea of people ready to engulf me like a wave breaking on the beach. It was my first day of school in second grade and my *first* trip on the school bus. Little did I know, that was the first of over *2,000* trips on that bus between second and eighth grade. It's safe to say I learned a few things.

That day I got on the bus and sat down, mildly unsure of myself, but confident I would survive. See, I was a little kid. Picture this: big glasses, highwater pants, a high-pitched voice and bucked teeth. I was a walking cartoon just ready to be made fun of. In the back of my mind, I knew I was a little different. I knew kids might want to make fun of me, but I had some protection. My older cousin rode the bus with me and he was in eighth grade. You wouldn't dare mess with an eighth grader, especially my older cousin. I may have been dorky, but I was protected...so it seemed.

My parents didn't think I would get the same quality education in the inner city that I would in the suburbs, so they chose to send me to a private Christian school, called The Christian Academy. Going to school there from 2nd through 12th grade gave me a strong moral foundation that I wouldn't trade for the world. Little did they know, going to school out there, and riding the school bus, would eventually provide its own unique set of "problems". I also had a best friend that rode the bus with me. Our parents had been friends for a long time so that made us more than just acquaintances, that made us friends. **Acquaintances** are people you spend time with on occasion; someone you're getting to know, but you don't know them that well. They have the potential to become a friend. A **friend** is a person you share a strong relationship with. It has been built over time. You consider this person *reliable* and *empathetic* which are two strong character traits in a friend.

# CRITICAL THINKING

**Why is it important to know the difference between "friends" and "acquaintances"?**

_____

_____

_____

_____

_____

_____

_____

_____

_____

_____

_____

_____

_____

_____

_____

_____

_____

At any age, but especially when you're a teen, it's important to understand the difference between friends and acquaintances. I want to tackle this early, because more than anything, who you spend your time with greatly affects your character.

In many situations, when kids are in school they tend to call those near them, "friends". By near, I mean close proximity. This may be someone who lives in the same neighborhood, someone who rides the same bus, sits at the same lunch table, or even sits next to them in class. They may frequently share surface level, meaningless information, but that does not make a friend. My friend and I sat next to each other on the bus every day. We made our seat, for that entire hour-long bus ride, our own personal, imaginary world. We didn't care about anything. It's what I like to call, "The carefree lifestyle".

Between the ages of 4 and 8, most kids live in the stage of the "carefree lifestyle". It's that stage in your life where the only thing that can seem to stop you is your own imagination. It's that time in your life before you begin to really care or notice what other people are thinking about you. It's that time in your life when you were able to **BELIEVE IN YOURSELF AND YOUR ABILITY TO DO YOUR BEST.** It was before the pressures of class and the unfair expectations of life got to you. I can remember being young and having confidence in everything I did, and if I hadn't done it yet, I was willing to try. Do you remember those days? Living the "carefree lifestyle" allows you to live your best life and put your best foot forward.

All my friend and I cared about was playing with Ninja Turtles. Yes, Teenage Mutant Ninja Turtles, along with spelling and vocabulary words and Saturday morning cartoons (You may not be old enough to know about "Saturday morning cartoons", so go find someone with a few gray hairs, and ask them). I was too young to be aware of or even care much about what people thought about me. But I also went to a school where I felt safe from danger, or so I thought. Much of second grade went on without a hitch. I was introduced to a new school, made new friends, and got through an entire year just as a second grader should, happily.

Every year school would let out, and for me, that could mean only one thing: visiting my aunt for the summer. My parents worked every day, which meant that I spent my summers visiting my aunt in Kentucky. I loved going to see my aunt. For a month, instead of busy city streets, it was quiet suburban neighborhoods. In place of litter and stray cats, were clean sidewalks and manicured lawns. It was like going to a whole new world. It made me feel different. Safe. Traveling there made me view life differently. It made me believe that I didn't have to live my life in just one place. It made me believe that I could and would experience more, I just didn't know it yet.

**"The purpose of life is to live it, to taste experience to the utmost, to reach out eagerly and without fear for newer and richer experience."**

**— Eleanor Roosevelt**
**(Former First Lady)**

# DID YOU KNOW...

You are the sum of all your life experiences. Meaning, if you add up all the things that have ever happened to you, and then considered how you reacted to them, that is how you got to be who you are. That is how you developed your character. Both good and bad experiences happen to everyone, it's how you deal with that determines your character. But remember this; where you are now is not where you are going, and if you are not happy with your progress, you can change it. Every day is a new opportunity. Wake up today knowing you can be better than you were yesterday.

# NOTES

# Chapter 2

## LEARNING THE ROPES

Fast forward to sixth grade, middle school. Life is fun when you don't have a care in the world. Much of my early elementary school days were that way, care-free. Middle school was the complete opposite, as I became much more aware of my skills and abilities and what I could do in the classroom. Don't tell anyone this, but do you know what I realized in middle school? I realized that I not only loved math, I was good at it. But I couldn't tell anyone because you don't want anyone to know. Or at least that's how it felt in sixth grade. I felt like I was going to be made fun of for being good at math. What sense does that make? Do you sometimes hide your greatness to try to make others feel adequate?

I remember the first time this insecurity crept up on me. It was something I never felt before. See, sixth grade was the first time anyone made fun of me just for being different, but I wasn't sure what was *THAT* different about me. I'm guessing they called me a "nerd" because of the combination of big "Bottle-cap" glasses and my pants that refused to be found anywhere near my shoes. They used to call those highwaters. "The flood is gone, the land is dry, why in the world are your pants so high?" Many adults, especially teachers, who caught up in the rigor of the day, simply refer to this as "teasing". While we refer to it as "teasing", this tends to minimize the act. Though it was only teasing, those words changed the trajectory of my life forever. I write about them today.

I was hearing statements like this directed at me on the way to school and coming home. When these things are being said to you, they make you "feel" like you are less than what you are but that is not true. Often, those who make fun of others are doing so to make up for insecurities in their own lives. I learned the importance of surrounding yourself with people who will affirm and celebrate the positive qualities in you; sometimes even bringing out qualities you didn't know you had.

# Lesson #2

# You are Fearfully and Wonderfully made

Never let anyone define who you are but you. You were meant to be who you are, and you have a purpose. The Bible tells us in Psalm 139:14a, *"I praise you because I am fearfully and wonderfully made..."* Nothing about you is a mistake in any way. Embrace who you are as an individual, because you were created with a specific purpose in mind.

**List some positive adjectives that describe who you are (Ex. Compassionate):**

- _____

- _____

- _____

- _____

- _____

- _____

Describe a time when you have felt most successful in your life. Why did you feel successful?

_____

_____

_____

_____

_____

_____

_____

_____

_____

_____

THE FEELING I REMEMBER MOST was not knowing how to respond to people when they talked about me. I remember being told to ignore them, and the old, "sticks and stones may break my bones". Well...words do hurt. They can make you *feel* inadequate. In fact, it has been the things that people have said to me that have hurt more than any physical pain. Sure enough, like many kids who share the same experience, I became more reserved and answered fewer and fewer questions as the year went on, because words do hurt. I went from a bright, outgoing, passionate little boy, to a shy, reserved, and insecure boy who didn't know his place.

*In my mind*, I was meant to be the coolest kid to walk the earth, speaking confidently, looking people in the eye, and treating others the way I wanted to be treated. But where I grew up, and in many communities, showing respect isn't *always* the way to earn respect. In fact, on Bus 23, I quickly learned that the only way to "have fun" and "protect yourself" is to make fun at the expense of others. Little did I know, the innocence of childhood, would be replaced by the guilt of adolescent behavior.

# CRITICAL THINKING

How can the way an individual is treated at a young age, affect their character later?  In what ways has your character been affected by what people have said to you?  Both positively and negatively.

_____

_____

_____

_____

_____

_____

_____

_____

_____

_____

_____

_____

_____

_____

_____

Popularity is an illusion of the mind, created by adolescent teenagers to determine where they fit in the larger community. Unfortunately for kids, popularity is directly related to how much they value themselves. Being popular means you are valued in the eyes of your peers. It has nothing to do with how *you* feel about yourself. This goes back to the ideas of **Self-Esteem and Self-Concept.** The negativity I faced, and that many kids face in school, causes them to look outwardly (Extrinsically) for motivation or affirmation rather than inwardly (Intrinsically) for their motivation.

The problem with motivation is that if it isn't coming from you, it can be inconsistent. The world provides a constant bombardment of obstacles for you to face. Setting personal goals will help keep you focused and provide the intrinsic motivation you need to ignore and avoid negativity. Of course, I understand the feelings of wanting to be social and popular in school. Sometimes, the cost of success is popularity.

# Lesson #3

# Intrinsic vs. Extrinsic Motivation

**Extrinsic motivation** is a form of external motivation. Many times, the motivation comes from a tangible reward a person may receive for completing the task. For example, a person may work harder on a job for a bonus. Extrinsic motivation can be good for immediate response towards meeting a goal, but is not sustainable because tangible rewards lose meaning, or may not always be available.

**Intrinsic motivation** is an internal form of motivation and based more on self-achievement rather than external rewards. For example, an employee may stay late on the job because of the sense of accomplishment you feel having done a good job. It is important to build your Intrinsic motivation which is more based on your values and is much more sustainable throughout your life.

ONE-WAY kids protect themselves against other kids is to talk about them, or "bust" on them. One of the more popular ways to make fun of someone is to tell a "Yo Mama" joke. These were the main types of jokes told on Bus 23. It was like a "rite of passage". The funnier your "Yo Mama" joke was, the cooler you were in the group. "Your mom is so...this" and "your mom is so...that!". Today, it remains yet another manner of insulting another student.

Now I don't know about you, but I love my mom, and never wanted anyone to talk about her. So, to prevent being the victim of these cruel jokes, I told them. Here I am, a sixth grader, talking about other people's mothers for fear that they would talk about mine. Every day on the bus became a moral battle. It became a daily stress, a conflict of my character. I had parents who spent time teaching me respect. I went to church, and to a school that talked every day about respecting your neighbor, but I struggled with thoughts of doing things I didn't believe in to have "friends" that I didn't even want, just to avoid conflict that I didn't otherwise know how to deal with.

Learning the ropes became damaging to my character. It was easy to see that the school bus could be the breeding ground for questionable behavior. Kids would do things like ball up and shoot soggy spitballs at each other. It takes until you learn character traits such as **empathy**, or putting yourself in someone else's shoes, where you learn that it isn't the kids who pay for shooting spitballs, it is the driver who has to clean it up. "Yo Mama" jokes became the norm, and more vulgar and sexual in nature. Young boys yelling out the window at young ladies and shooting rubber bands at pedestrians also became part of the daily activities. One kid put saliva on his fingers and rubbed them on my glasses like "windshield wipers". Who does that? Things on the bus had gotten so bad, that I would get off a few stops early just so I didn't have to deal with it. When "self-preservation" and "survival of the fittest" begin to set in, morals and values go out the window. When I wanted to join in so I wouldn't be the victim, my "friends" were nowhere to be found to encourage me to do the right thing, and I wasn't equipped with the skills to **Encourage myself when no one else would.** The only skill I was equipped with was assimilation, or accepting other ideas as my own. In short, I knew how to do what everyone else was doing, so I did.

Part of encouraging yourself is using daily affirmations to remind yourself of your purpose, abilities, and goals. While you are going through these daily experiences, you must equip yourself with the mindset to overcome those obstacles. Below is an affirmation I say with my class daily, to remind them of who they are and of what they are capable:

# SAY THIS TO YOURSELF DAILY WHEN YOU WAKE UP!

## MY DAILY AFFIRMATION

I BELIEVE IN MYSELF AND MY ABILITY TO DO MY BEST.

I AM INTELLIGENT.

I AM CAPABLE OF GREATNESS.

I CAN LEARN.  I WILL LEARN.  I MUST LEARN.

TODAY I WILL LISTEN.

I WILL SPEAK.

I WILL SEE.

I WILL FEEL.

I WILL REASON.

I WILL READ AND I WILL WRITE.

I WILL DO ALL THESE THINGS WITH ONE PURPOSE IN MIND.

TO DO MY BEST

I AM TOO SMART TO WASTE TODAY

# NOTES

# Chapter 3

# Times Get Rough

The following year, I returned to school, but now I was in seventh grade, and my thoughts and feelings were a little different. My mind was starting to fill with thoughts of things other than Ninja Turtles, and board games. I started to wonder if the girl who sat in my class was "pretty" or not. I started to wonder if she thought I was cute and what other people thought about me. This wasn't just a once-in-a-while thing. I was having these thoughts all the time, mixed in with a few math problems here and there if the teacher called on me.

Seventh grade was a tough year. Again, I didn't understand the why behind it until now. After two long difficult rides on the bus every day, I would come home and express my feelings to my parents. One of the messages that I regularly heard was, "don't be like those other kids. You are better than that." Those statements began to sink in as I started to see more and more behaviors on the bus that I didn't agree with. I often saw people that I respected the most do things that I thought were wrong. Being so young,

I had a hard time identifying who were good friends and who weren't. I lacked the self-esteem necessary to develop positive new relationships. This made it difficult to make friends, so anyone that I felt was interested in being a friend, I was all for it. In many instances in school, students are forced into friendships simply out of convenience.


Some say it's difficult to find true friends; that most people have ill-intentions and only look out for themselves. All I knew was that I didn't want to be the kid with no friends. Quickly, my relationships with my peers became more important than my morals and what I felt was right and wrong. Suddenly, I was willing to risk getting in trouble just to maintain what I thought was a friendship.

# CRITICAL THINKING

What are traits you look for in a good friend? Why are those traits important to you?

_____

_____

_____

_____

_____

_____

_____

_____

_____

_____

_____

_____

_____

_____

_____

_____

_____

_____

While reading more about friendships, I learned that two-character traits a person should look for in a good friend are **reliability** and **empathy**. When a friend is reliable, you can count on them to have your best interest at heart in every situation. An empathetic friend is always able to see things from your point of view and put themselves in your situation. I was young when I realized that most people aren't reliable, and they certainly don't care about your feelings or situation. But that's just MOST people. Then you come across ones that do care. Keep your eye out for those. Those are the same people who will like you for you, and no other reason.

When I talk to my students and mentees about their friendships, and one is having trouble, it is typically over a lack of trust or an incidence of distrust. Many teenagers have not identified **trust** as an important value. Trust is temporary and based on the importance of the relationship. The more important the relationship, the more trust there is. Teenagers fall victim to the **conditional friendship**; a friendship solely based on the convenience and the benefit of one or both "friends". *Conditional friendships* lead to distrust and negativity. Middle school was full of those types of relationships. Many of my acquaintances, people who rode my school bus, were becoming conditional friends, people I couldn't count on, bringing distrust and negativity to my life.

"A healthy friendship is one where you share your true feelings without fearing the end of the relationship."

~Rachel Simmons (American Author)

# NOTES

# CHAPTER 4

# WHATEVER YOU DO...BE YOU!

Sixth and seventh grade were two of the most challenging years I had in school. Why? Because as I got older, the approval of people on the bus was important to me. What they thought about me seemed to be the only thing that mattered. When they asked me to do something, I did it, without thinking: Simply for approval. I continued to lack the confidence I needed to build my self-esteem and development a strong sense of self-concept.

One day, I got on the bus in seventh grade, and one of the students had a box of pencils he had brought in from home. The things we could do with pencils were endless. We could have pencil wars, act like we were doing karate and chop them with our hands, but today, we decided to live on the edge. After we broke our pencils, someone had the bright idea of throwing them out of the window into moving cars. *Of course*, this went against *everything* I believed. Now, I don't remember the exact thoughts I had when I chose to participate in this nonsense, but I promise you, it was all about getting the approval of my peers. And there was nothing more important to me than approval…right?

As the bus ride went on, all the kids seemed to be having fun breaking their pencils and throwing them out the window at unsuspecting pedestrians and drivers. There was certainly the little angel on my right shoulder saying, "didn't you go to church on Sunday?" And on my left shoulder was the tiny little devil asking me, "don't you want to fit in with the rest of the kids?" Before I tell you what I did, this is the perfect time to teach the lesson in the story because this is the time where you need to think before you act.

The only things that would have saved me in that situation were the values that I had established in my life until that point. If I would have **taken my time and made the best decision** based on my values, I would have avoided the situation. In my mind, there was a very good chance that if I did not throw a pencil out the window at some point that I would either be made fun of, or even worse, bullied for the remainder of the year, simply because I didn't share the same values as my peers. Simply having a second thought about throwing the pencil were my values kicking in. But what did I do?

Not wanting to miss out on the fun, I proceeded to do the same. I grabbed my pencil and dramatically broke it in half, prepared to launch it out the window like the baseball player I was. One kid, like 4th down of the super bowl, encouraged me saying, "Yea Dev! You got this!" With my palms sweaty, knees weak, arms heavy, I wound up, and threw my pencil out the window; hurling it towards the driver in the car. As the pencil entered his window, I saw him look up to identify where it came from. I ducked down in my seat as quickly as I could trying not to be seen, and all my "friends" did the same. The driver of the car slowly pulled around to the other side of the bus to talk to the bus driver about what happened. I could see the driver frantically waving his finger pointing to my side of the bus. As the angry driver pulled away, our bus driver yelled to the back of the bus, "who threw that pencil?! As soon as I find out, you're off this bus!" Immediately, all the people that I thought were my friends, quickly became conditional friends, and turned and pointed to me. I felt betrayed by who I thought were friends. The same people I threw the pencil to impress, "dimed me out". This was one of the most embarrassing moments of my life. I quickly realized that I didn't have real friends, only conditional friends and "real friends" are hard to come by. Not to mention, I would be kicked off the bus and lose the trust of my parents.

The biggest disappointment of this incident was that it was by far one of the worst things I had ever done. It was the first time my actions put someone else at risk. It's always easy to look back on your mistake and wish you never did it, but where kids struggle is taking the time to think before they act.

# CRITICAL THINKING

Describe a time when you blatantly went against your values and did something you did not agree with. (Don't say you don't have any either)

_____

_____

_____

_____

_____

_____

_____

_____

_____

_____

_____

_____

_____

_____

_____

_____

_____

_____

_____

# NOTES

# Chapter 5

# Who Do you Want to be?

Read the title to this chapter to yourself three times and ask yourself, "Who do you want to be?" Have you ever thought about this? Have you ever thought about who you are? If someone were to walk up to you right now and ask "Who are you?" What would the answer be?

When I ask adolescents, or young people between the age of 10-17 the question, "Who are you?", it often goes unanswered or the question is simply met with a basic answer, their name. Why is that? Why are teens unable to articulate who they are?

To adolescents, the belief about who or what you are is concrete. The idea that an individual is ever-changing, and evolving has not yet set in. When I ask a student, "Who are you?", I get a name, and when I ask "What are you?", I get an ability, like "basketball player", "gymnast", "singer", or "dancer". Teens have a very concrete view of their self-concept. Through growth, maturity, and a true understanding that you are meant to be different, teens can develop a strong positive self-concept.

Self-concept is created by our daily experiences and interactions with others. One of the most important changes that occurs during teenage years involves the development of the self-concept, or the belief of who you are, and the development of new relationships. While most younger children are strongly attached to their parents, teens move increasingly away from their parents and towards their peers. As a result, parents have less and less influence on their children. This can be dangerous when kids are spending considerably more time with their peers than their parents. For me, it was even more of a struggle because of the two hours a day I spent on the school bus.

Now, although much of this book is about my struggles on the bus, it's important to remind you that, "Where you are now, is not where you are going." Something clicked for me. At the beginning of eighth grade, something told me that who I had been trying to be for the last two years, simply wasn't me.

I remember my mindset changing as I developed confidence in who I was. Being an eighth grader on the bus meant I was the oldest one. It meant there was no more bullying, and I could learn to be the best version of myself: unapologetically. One thing that also helped my self-confidence was participation in extra-curricular activities. In seventh grade, I played three games on the basketball team because of poor grades. I decided in eighth grade, that I would play the entire season. I also joined the chess club. To some reading this book, it may sound "nerdy", or even "too difficult" to learn, which is the very thing I thought right before I learned. But chess changed me. Chess helped to direct mis-guided energy and taught me patience and forward thinking. Lastly, I joined the choir. Many of us enjoy singing casually to ourselves for relaxation or self-expression. Joining the choir put me in a room with like-minded people with the same goal; to make beautiful music. Choir provided me a sense of freedom and self-expression that I never had. Eventually, music and sports became my identity at The Christian Academy.

Music and sports weren't my only extra-curricular activities. On the school bus was where I met my first girlfriend. Don't get me wrong. It was your typical middle school relationship, shy and awkward at times. But like your typical middle school boy, I struggled with boundaries and what was "cute" or bordering "inappropriate".

I remember sharing with students in my class about "level II" detentions at The Christian Academy. Of course, like inquisitive middle schoolers, they wanted to know more about these…detentions. So, I told them. Level II detentions are two hours long, and cost $10. In shock, they all began to murmur amongst the group. I explained to them that we received those types of reprimands for infractions such as "hugging", and because of that discipline, it prevented a lot of issues that arise from blurred lines of what is appropriate versus inappropriate behavior. I am thankful for such discipline instilled in me at a young age. What seemed like a burden then, ended up being a blessing.

This book is about my struggles with trying to decide who I wanted to be and how I viewed myself. As a child, again and again, I was put in situations that caused me to doubt myself. Much of the advice that I and many kids get is to "ignore the situation and it will go away". As a mature adult, but more importantly, an experienced educator, I realize the importance of providing young people with concrete strategies to overcome these obstacles.

# NOTES

# CHAPTER 6

# B.E.T. ON YOURSELF

Even as you read this book, life will continue to throw you difficult choices and decisions to make. Every day, you are faced with decisions and choices that will dictate who you grow up to be. Every decision you make has a consequence. The way you view yourself, your behavioral choices, and the people you associate with will all greatly affect your character. It is my goal to ensure that you have some concrete strategies to help you overcome the adversity, particularly the peer pressures of life.

Below are three easy steps to help you build a strong sense of self-esteem and a positive self-concept. I believe a strong sense of self-esteem and a positive self-concept lead to strong character. "BET" on yourself to ensure your own success:

*B* - **Believe in yourself and your ability to do your best.** You are fearfully and wonderfully made, and you were created with a specific purpose in mind. You've been given a dream in your heart. Pursuing that dream is the very thing that will give you the confidence to deal with adversity. Your purpose is the very thing that drives you, that wakes you up every day, and pushes you to do more with yourself. Tap into that inner self. Tap into that inner being that wants a little more. It's not easy, I know. When I was in fifth grade, in our Bible class, we had to memorize the entire book of James in the Bible. It has 5 chapters, and we had to learn five verses every week. James says, "Consider it pure joy, my brothers, whenever you face trials of any kind. Because you know that the testing of your faith develops perseverance. Perseverance must finish its work, so that you may be mature and complete, not lacking anything." Embrace your chase, because after the struggle comes amazing grace.

E - **Encourage yourself when no one else will.** So many people are going to tell you that you can't do something, be something, come up with a "Plan B", or try to convince you that you are less than what you are. Remember that your dream is powerful enough to not only push you, but change the world if you let it.  Never let the fear of someone else's opinion prevent you from reaching *your* goals.  Even as I write this book, the patience it takes to get all your thoughts out, and encourage others to be their best self, can be difficult to find, but the only thing that carries me on is you; the person reading this book.

**T** – **Take Your Time, Make the Best Decision.**  My father used to say every decision you make has a consequence.  Most bad decisions are made hastily, and alone.  Sometimes, it's time, that allows you to talk yourself into bad decisions.  Surround yourself with five good people until learning to navigate relationships is second nature.  This is where strong, reliable and empathic people in your corner can help to ensure you are making the best decision by giving every decision the time it deserves.

It has been my pleasure to share my life experiences on the school bus with you, and I can only hope that the events and lessons that have been shared with you equip you with the skills to overcome negative circumstances in your life and help you move toward being the best version of yourself. Although the school bus was the place that provided me with a number of life lessons, there may be another similar place in your life that provides the same experiences, your own Bus 23. Look for the opportunities in every situation to learn, because they are there if you seek them out. I believe you can do anything you set out to do with all your heart, just remember to F.O.C.U.S. because "Finding Ourselves Creates Unlimited Success".

# NOTES

# Chapter 7

# S.M.A.R.T. Goal Setting Worksheet

Now, I'll be honest with you. It can be hard to muster up the will power to sit down and write out goals for yourself. I am speaking from experience. It has always been difficult for me to stop and do things that seem tedious, partly because I always felt that there were other things I'd rather be or could be doing. I mean, why write down my goals if I could just take action towards it and save time?

Many of us have great intentions. We intend on accomplishing the things we want most out of life, but then what happens? Life gets in the way! You have an unexpected assignment in school. A family emergency comes up. Next thing you know, you are back to doing things without a purpose, without a "why". Writing goals down allows you to keep them in the forefront of your mind, causing your positive energy and actions to flow towards making that goal a reality. It also reminds you that you have a purpose when life makes you feel like what's important to you is unimportant to everyone else. Having objectives allows you to clearly identify exactly what you have to do to accomplish your goal and clearly see when you have moved closer or not.

I have created a simple, yet effective goal setting exercise and worksheet below to assist you in laying a foundation for achieving your goals. Check it out on the next page.

# Directions:

Use this worksheet below to create **short-term** and **long-term goals** as well as **objectives** for yourself. I believe with a simple written plan, you will be well on your way to achieving the things you want in life.

As you create this plan, I want you to think BIG. Most people don't think big, because they tell themselves in their minds that they can't have it. But you achieve anything God wants for you, if you truly put the work necessary into achieving it. Think about what you truly want and create a plan, a set of goals to get it. You will set two sets of goals; Short-Term Goals and Long-Term Goals, with a set of 2-3 objectives, or small steps, to achieve those goals.

Your short-term goals should lead to the achievement of your long-term goals. But, it's not good enough to just write goals. They must be S.M.A.R.T. goals that, when written, can transform your life. S.M.A.R.T. stands for:

- S – SPECIFIC

- M – MEASURABLE

- A – ATTAINABLE

- R – REALISTIC

- T – TIMELY

# Directions: Circle the Correct Answer

*Specific* goals are detailed and allow you to see the end completed.

- "I want to be fast"

- "I want to be the fastest runner in my class"


*Measurable* goals allow to goal-setter to see when the goal is completed. By writing a measurable goal, you can see when you have completed your goal. This most important to the completion of your goals.

- I want to do well in school this year

- I want to have a 3.5 GPA this year


*Attainable* goals ensure that the goal-setter is working towards something they can achieve without getting discouraged along the way.

- I want to make honor roll this quarter

- I want to get A's on every assignment this quarter


*Realistic* Goals remind the goals-setter to set goals that are within their reach.

- I want to travel the world

- I want to travel to 4 countries every year


*Timely* goals remind the goal-setter to attach and end to the completion of the goal.

- I want to own a home

- I want to buy a home by age 18

**Objectives** are small steps you can take to achieving a goal you have

- Short Term Goal: I want to get an "A" in math during the first quarter
    - o Objective: I am going to do my HW every night during the first quarter
    - o Objective: I am going to stay after school for tutoring twice per week

On the next page, take time to identify some short term and long-term goals for yourself:

# Example:

Long Term Goal #1: Positively Affect the Lives of 1 Million Youth

Objective #1: Write a book in the next 30 days

Short Term Goal #1: Write a book entitled Bus 23 in the next 30 days

Objective #1: Write a Chapter every night for 5 nights

| Long Term Goal #1 | Objective #1 |
| --- | --- |
|  |  |

| Short Term Goal #1 | Objective #1 |
| --- | --- |
|  |  |

| Long Term Goal #2 | Objective #2 |
| --- | --- |
|  |  |

| Short Term Goal #2 | Objective #2 |
| --- | --- |
|  |  |

"Who you are right now might just be good enough, but who you'll grow to be, may change the world"

~ Devon "Coach" Buchanan

# About the Author:

My name is Devon Buchanan. I am a native of Southwest Philadelphia, Pennsylvania. Having been raised in a God-fearing family, and attending Christian school for 11 years, much of my understanding is rooted in the Christian faith, although the principles in this book can be applied to anyone's life.

I attended East Stroudsburg University of Pennsylvania where I received a B.S. in Recreation and Leisure Services Management. My college experience helped me develop a love for youth development and enrichment. I spent much of my early professional years working for the

YMCA and local government agencies in youth recreation positions before transitioning to education.

I began teaching in 2009 at one of the top performing charter networks in the nation, North Star Academy in Newark, NJ. It was there where I not only developed a passion for educating youth, but a skill for connecting with youth on both an academic and personal level. Returning to Philadelphia, and logging thousands of hours of face-to-face interaction over the course of 7 years as a Physical Education teacher with students of all of ages and cultural backgrounds, led me to pursue my M.A. in Multicultural Education. I understand that if I learn more about culture and how young people learn, I can positively affect the lives of youth all over the world using both education and recreation as a vehicle.

As I progress in my career, my goal is to positively affect the lives of one million youth while opening a network of youth recreation centers all over the world. Bus 23 is my way to using my personal experiences to positively affect the lives of everyone who reads it.  I hope, in some fashion, I have done that.

If you have been blessed by this book in any way, I invite you to follow my journey on social media and supporting my organization, The F.O.C.U.S. Youth Network, Inc.  F.O.C.U.S. stands for "Finding Ourselves Creates Unlimited Success" because I truly believe that providing our with extraordinary experiences with produce extraordinary individuals.  We provide innovative educational and recreational activities for youth and their families centered around Wellness and Nutrition Education, Character Development, and Post-Secondary Success.  I thank you and appreciate all your support!

Yours in Christ,

Devon "Coach" Buchanan

## Social Media:

[f] Focus Youth Network

[◎] @CoachCannon215

[◎] @FocusYouthNetwork

www.ingramcontent.com/pod-product-compliance
Lightning Source LLC
LaVergne TN
LVHW010034070426
835509LV00004B/143